Not nice

Open oyster

Paint the pail

Quilt a quilt

Rubber raft

Smelly shoe

Trollusk tears

Usually unlucky

Very vain vampire

Wash the walrus

Xray

Your yellow yarn

Zipperump-a-zoo

run

leap

hop

Table of Contents

climb

read

rest

crawl

fly

walk

fall

Little Monster's Word Book

By

Mercer Mayer

MERRIGOLD PRESS • NEW YORK

Library of Congress Catalog Card Number: 76-55118   ISBN: 0-307-11022-2   A MCMXCI

dive

slip

skip

tumble

washboard

washtub bass

COUNTRY AND WESTERN BAND

bow

fiddle

kazoo

guitar

harmonica

five-string banjo

Cowboy CRITTER and his WACKY WACKY BAND

e

drumsticks

batons

parade snare drum

baton twirlers

drum major

Music

roller coaster

County Fair

barn

silo

trac[tor]

prize tomato

farmer

rooster

BUMPER CARS

cow

goat

sheep

horse

RIDE THE DONKEY AND GET YOUR PICTURE TAKEN

SHOOTING GALLERY

HIT THE BOTTLE

Teddy bea[r]

pinwheel

milk bottles

camera

cotton candy

8

photographer

win-a-prize booths

Ferris wheel

TEST YOUR MUSCLES

bell

nwheel

HOME MADE

cake   bread   pie

jams and jellies

mallet

Catch a Greased Kerploppus

RIDE A KERPLOPPUS MERRY-GO-ROUND

cone

cotton candy seller

ice cream

scale

50 60 70
40   80
30   90
20   100
  10

I WILL GUESS YOUR WEIGHT OR YOU WIN A BEAN BAG

foot-long hot dog

TICKETS

weight-guessing trollusk

ticket booth

thunder lizard
(brontosaurus)

little
kitty cat

big kitty cat

This big bird is
called a pterodactyl.
I bet you a piece
of bubble gum you
can't say that.

That!

parrot

fish

goldfish

flea

cricket

hamster

white mice

10

The Great Pet Show

pet bat

pet flower

lizard

turtle

zipperump-a-zoo

pet ake

worm

puppy fydolagump

t-prize bon

pet shoe

puppy dog

pet-judging trollusk

(If you were the judge, who would get first prize?)

bone

11

Games

catcher's mask
catcher
bat
baseball?

ball

batter

mitt

BASEBALL

pitcher

bird

JACKS jacks

winner

CHECKERS

loser

checkers

checkerboard

birdie

racket

net

hoop

net

BADMINTON

basketball

croquet ball

wicket

mallet

CROQUET

BASKETBALL

hide

12

pins

bowling ball

BOWLING

bowler

CARDS

football

catch

Who is right?

GUESSING

seeker

"it"

TAG

target

shooter

kick

helmet

dart

ring

MARBLES

FOOTBALL

AND SEEK

DARTS

13

Things to Do With Paper

FOLD IT

hat

paper airplane

CUT IT

paper doll chain

scissors

scraps (throw them away)

newspaper

WAD IT UP

DRAW A PICTURE

crayon

pencil

ballpoint pen

MAKE A MASK

MAKE A PAPER CHAIN

WRITE A LETTER

Dear Bill, can you read yet.

paper with lines

string to tie it on

crayon

scissors (always be careful with scissors)

clothespins

rope

construction paper or cardboard

flashlight

paste

PASTE A PICTURE

sheet

MAKE A SHADOW-PUPPET SHOW

tape

stick

shadow puppet

MAKE A FLOWER

heavy paper or cardboard

Birthday Party

balloons

paper lanterns

egg-and-spoon race

punch bowl

ladle

egg

sack race

camera

party hat

noise-makers

candles

birthday boy

birthday cake

paper cup

party favor

bowl

plate

fork

Pin the Tail on the Kerploppus

shirt

presents

tablecloth

jigsaw puzzle

ice cream and cake

15

Spooky Times

bat

looking for
something
in the attic

What is your favorite
spooky time?

moon

clouds

hearing the
wind howl

owl

passing
an empty house

watching a
scary TV show

looking
for something
in the
cellar

taking out
the garbage

furnace

mouse

Weather

snowflakes

raindrops

hailstones

umbrella

icicles

RAIN

HAIL

SNOW

SUNNY

lightning

beach

FOG

THUNDERSTORM

TORNADO

WINDY

17

hot dog

hot-dog-
snatching bombanat

tree house

bird

butterfly

lean-to

outdoor
fireplace

CAMPING

flashlight

camper

backpack

canteen

sleeping

hatchet

tent

ants

cattails

anthill

radio

picnic basket

rowboat

oar

Thermos
bottle

frog

cold milk

lily pad

bench

picnic table

PICNIC

18

Summertime

kite

kite string

turning somersaults

HAY RIDE

fishing pole

can of worms

swimming trunks

bathing cap

FISHING

nming

WATER SKIING

diving board

water skis

mast

sail

SWIMMING

BOATING

sailboat

pond

19

T-shirt flag

snow castle

ski lift

snow

snow shovel

SLEDDING

gloves

jacket

sled

SNOWBALL FIGHT

top hat

snowballs

sticks

ice fangs

Thermos bottle

hot chocolate

figure skates

BUILDING A
SNOW MONSTER

ICE SKATING

20

Wintertime

SLEIGH RIDE

ski
poles

skis

SKIING

ski
boots

icicles

ICE HOCKEY

hockey
stick

mittens

hole

line

fish

puck

snowsuit

bench

ICE FISHING

mast

sail

boots

earmuffs

stocking cap

scarf

frozen pond

ICE BOATING

runner

21

Holidays

HALLOWEEN

witch

false nose

candy bags

devil

skeleton jack o'lantern

VALENTINE'S DAY

hearts

red paper paper lace

paste

scissors

Make your own valentine!

THANKSGIVING

blunderbuss

roast turkey

pumpkin pie

Pilgrim

Pilgrim

turkey

EASTER

Easter-bunny suit

dyeing eggs

yellow green

red

eggs

purple

chocolate bunny

jelly beans Easter basket

22

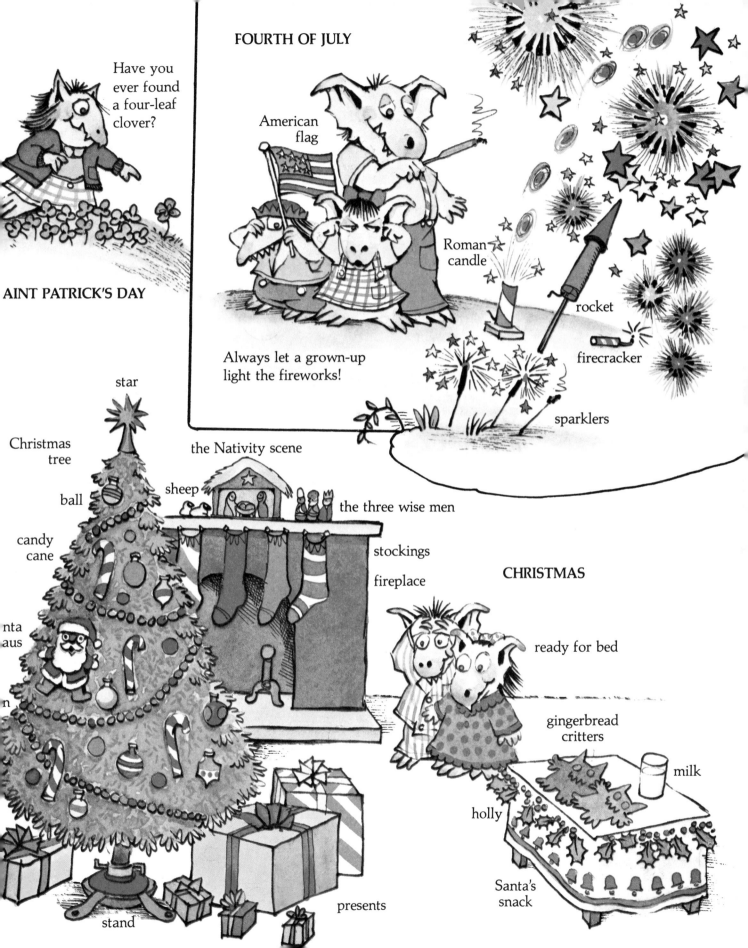

Have you ever found a four-leaf clover?

AINT PATRICK'S DAY

FOURTH OF JULY

American flag

Roman candle

rocket

firecracker

sparklers

Always let a grown-up light the fireworks!

star

Christmas tree

the Nativity scene

ball

sheep

the three wise men

candy cane

stockings

fireplace

CHRISTMAS

nta aus

ready for bed

gingerbread critters

milk

holly

Santa's snack

presents

stand

Ways to Travel

FREE BURGERS TODAY ONLY AT PETE'S PLACE

YOU'LL LIKE THEM

GET 'UM WHILE THEY LAST

WELCOME

Island Joe's RENT-A-TRAILER

END OF THE LINE

use your wings

helicopter

sailboat

paper cup

Pete

motorcycle

raft

unicycle

car

house trailer

bus

red wagon

tricycle

baby buggy

bicycle

by hands

24

balloon

UFO

jet

tugboat

rowboat

oar

rubber horse

vim

submarine

canoe

by elephant

paddle

by wheels

diesel train

EDGE OF NOWHERE OR BUST

on horseback

covered wagon

by feet

footprints

25

Moving Day

new friends

MONSTER MOVERS

GOLDEN

ask about our low rates

moving van

BOY, OH BOY, OH BOY, WOW!

SEAL OF GOODNESS

WE WILL MOVE YOU OR A ZOO ANYWHERE ANY TIME ANY PLACE EVEN TO THE EDGE OF NOWHERE

VAN WE ARE GOOD

sofa

picture

rabbit ears

hand truck

ramp

UP

moving carton

Have you ever rolled downhill in an empty moving carton?

grandfather clock

vacuum cleaner

antique table

lamp

boxes of books

potted palm

chimney

roof

old radio

old picture frames

dress form

steamer trunk

ATTIC

BEDROOM

light switch

pillow

mattress

bed

box of toys

BEDROOM

mover

iron

radiator

mirror

dresser

wastebasket

record player

LIVING ROOM

rug

mantel

fireplace

chair

ck

DINING ROOM

hanging the drapes

dining table

chair

KITCHEN

unpacking the dishes

pans

refrigerator

stove

spade

ng ard

rocking chair

skateboard

27

Secret Hiding Places

under the covers

in the closet

under the bed

behind the sofa

in the dark

in the sofa

behind the curtains

behind a chair

under a newspaper

under a lamp shade

OUTSIDE

in a bush

behind a tree

in a blanket tent

in a hollow tree trunk

behind a rock

in a hole
in the ground

in a cardboard
carton clubhouse

under the
porch steps

NOT in the
garbage can

29

lawn mower

rake

nozzle

hose

MOWING THE GRASS

RAKING LEAVES

WATERING THE FLOWER

sponge

hedge clipper

WASHING THE CAR

pail

TRIMMING THE HEDGE

dishes

Helping

HANGING UP YOUR CLOTHES

coat han

closet

SETTING THE TABLE

PUTTING AWAY YOUR BOOKS

bookcase

TYING LITTLE BROTHER'S SHOES

head of the bed

MAKING THE BED

broom

CLEANING UP YOUR ROOM

toy chest

foot of the bed

Feelings

happy　　　　jealous　　　　sad

selfish

sharing

greedy

mad

First Times

first letter

first fish

first A

first bull's-eye

first electric
train set

first telephone call

first home run

first camp-out

first tooth
to come out

first bicycle

first puppy

Things to Do or Be When You Get Bigger

farmer

truck driver

firefighter

police officer

doctor

gas station attendant

baker

storekeeper

astronaut

mail carrier

skin diver

photographer

artist

author

telephone operator

librarian

dentist

cabinetmaker

optician

florist

bird watcher

general

veterinarian

sailor

pilot

animal trainer

waiter

magician

juggler

taxi driver

actor   actress

hobo

35

Lessons

sheet music

SINGING

PIANO

tutu

toe shoes

BALLET

tap shoe

TAP

KARATE

swimming trunks

SWIMMING

hunting cap

saddle

reins

bridle

RIDING

mask

fencing swords

chest protector

FENCING

TENNIS

tennis ball

tennis racket

net

intbrush

nvas

model

easel

palette

PAINTING

POTTERY

potter's wheel

SCULPTURE

beret

smock

CLAY

sculpting tools

VIOLIN

BAGPIPE

COOKING

pan

spoon

apron

mixing bowl

GROWL

SNEER   BOO

SCARING LESSONS

37

Colors

RED

mix:

RED
+
YELLOW
ORANGE

plaid

YELLOW

stripes

mix:

YELLOW
+
BLUE
GREEN

BLUE

check

waterfall

cave

fish

boulder

What color is: RED + BLUE ?

BROWN

Does red make
a bull angry?

Ask your parents
why the sky is blue.
Boy, will they have trouble
with that one!

rainbow

canary

bluejay

cardinal

tulips

roses

black-eyed
Susans

daffodils

bumblebee

poppies

Big and Little

Big and little,
Short and tall,
Fat and thin,
And that's not all.

Crooked and straight,
Round and square,
You can see something—
But nothing's not there.

40

For Your Head

king's crown

toupee

moustache

queen's crown

hair ribbon

eyeglasses

sunglasses

beard

wig

pith helmet

ponytail

chef's hat

football helmet

sailor hat

army helmet

earphones

baseball cap

catcher's mask

fire fighter's helmet

makeup

earrings

top hat

hummingbir

POWDER

bonnet

42

rubbers

baseball glove

knee socks

flippers

sneakers

roller skates

hiking boots

boxing gloves

high-heeled shoes

cowboy boots

mittens

ring

high-top sneakers

wooden shoes

nail polish

sandals

For Your Hands and Feet

argyle socks

gloves

snowshoes

rubber boots

fuzzy slippers

surfboard

stilts

pogo stick

slip

dress

undershirt

under pants

belt

necktie

bow tie

suit

vest

suspenders

trousers

turtleneck

blouse

necklace

bracelet

skirt

swimming suit

swimming trunks

shirt

tank top

shorts

hula hoop

T-shirt

bathrobe

For Your Middle

44

Dress-Up

helmet

sword

eye patch

water pistol

cowboy hat

COWBOY

banner

KNIGHT

deerstalker hat

cowboy boots

shield

PIRATE

magnifying glass

ten-gallon hat

headdress

bow and arrow

trench coat

bandana

INDIAN

DETECTIVE

BANDIT

hobby horse

scooter

MONSTER

MAD SCIENTIST

crown

test tubes

royal robe

flask

microscope

DADDY

MOMMY

laboratory coat

KING AND QUEEN

Boy is that a funny mask.

cape

SUPERHERO

That's no mask. It's my face.

45

Numbers

1 little thing

2 trollusks running

3 sleeping kerploppuses

4 peeping eyeballs

5 devils laughing

6 useless blobs

7 broken windows